Essentials
of *Kayak Touring*

by the American Canoe Association

ACA
AMERICAN CANOE ASSOCIATION
Kayak & Canoe Recreation

A book of this sort presents not the opinions of one person but rather the distilled wisdom and experience of many. Accordingly, in compiling it, we have benefited greatly from the ideas and suggestions of others. These debts are simply too numerous to name in full, so we resort to thanking only those whose services were especially noteworthy. Charlie Wilson and Patty Caruthers helped identify a need for this book and encouraged us to write it. Becky Molina, Kent Ford, and Mike Aronoff were helpful and generous reviewers whose suggestions made the text more clear and accurate. The book as a whole owes much to an American Canoe Association (ACA) textbook compiled by Pam Dillon. Dillon's work, in turn, owes much to Tom Foster's earlier writings. Menasha Ridge Press in general, and Russell Helms in particular, deserve thanks for their expertise. Alabama Small Boats has again provided significant material support. The Standards Committee of the Safety Education and Instruction Council reviewed the manuscript, offered valuable suggestions, and endorsed the book for use with ACA courses. To those other individuals who contributed their comments and their energies and who are not singled out here, we express our sincere gratitude.

Copyright © 2005 by The American Canoe Association
Printed in the United States of America
All Rights Reserved
Published by Menasha Ridge Press
First edition, first printing

Text and cover design by Travis Bryant
Photo credits:
    United States Coast Guard, p. 24: "Foul weather" and "Wind and waves"
    USCG Office of Boating Safety, p. 24: "Small fast vessels"
    United States Navy, p. 36; guided-missile destroyer *USS Milius* (DDG 69)
    Other photos by Russell Helms
Illustrations on p. 27 by Scott McGrew

Library of Congress Cataloging-in-Publication Data
Essentials of kayak touring/by the American Canoe Association.
p. cm.
ISBN 0-89732-585-0
1. Kayaking. I. American Canoe Association.

Disclaimer: Outdoor activities are an assumed risk sport. This book cannot take the place of appropriate instruction for paddling, swimming, or lifesaving techniques. Every effort has been made to make this guide as accurate as possible, but it is the ultimate responsibility of the paddler to judge his or her ability and act accordingly.

Menasha Ridge Press	American Canoe Association
2204 First Avenue South, Suite 102	7432 Alban Station Boulevard, Suite B-232
Birmingham, AL 35233	Springfield, VA 22150-2311
(205) 322-0439	(703) 451-0141
www.menasharidge.com	www.acanet.org

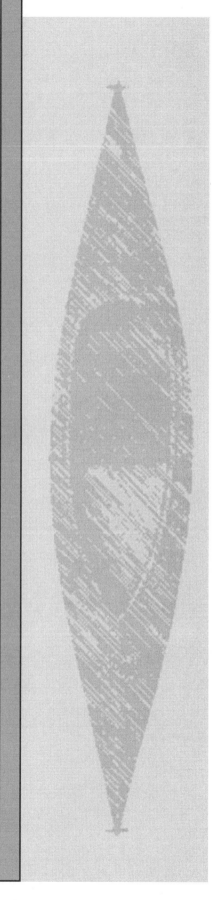

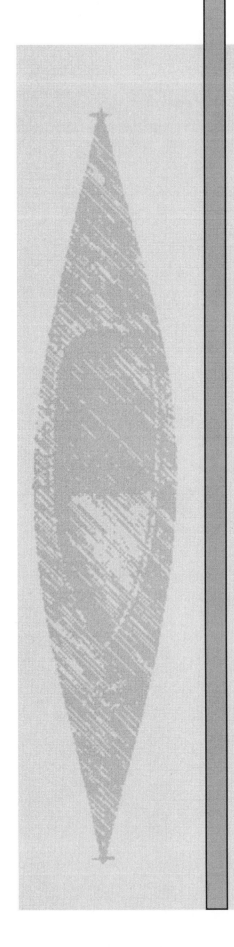

Foreword

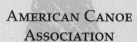

AMERICAN CANOE
ASSOCIATION

ESSENTIALS OF
KAYAK TOURING

Course Goals

Safety: To safely paddle on protected flatwater, perform self-rescue, and respond to emergencies.

Enjoyment: To become aware of paddling opportunities and the rewards of lifetime participation in paddling.

Skills: To acquire the ability to safely and enjoyably paddle on protected flatwater.

A nationwide nonprofit organization, the American Canoe Association (ACA) promotes paddlesport recreation and education and advocates for environmental stewardship of the nation's waterways. The ACA helps individuals and organizations understand how safe and positive paddling experiences can contribute to a higher quality of life. The ACA strives to make paddling education and instruction accessible to the public and to provide avenues for casual paddlers to become active paddlesport enthusiasts.

Safe, enjoyable paddling requires both knowledge and skill. This manual will help you gain both. If kayaking skills are developed with safety in mind, paddlers can have fun, enhance enjoyment of the sport, and enjoy the sport throughout their lifetimes.

In addition to reading this manual and practicing what you learn, we strongly recommend formal instruction from an ACA-certified instructor. ACA courses emphasize safety, enjoyment, and the development of paddling skills. Greater skills lead to greater fun and the ability to progress confidently to the next level of kayaking enjoyment.

I invite you to become a member of the American Canoe Association to share your joy of paddling on the waterways we all love.

Happy kayaking!

Pamela S. Dillon, Executive Director

American Canoe Association

7432 Alban Station Boulevard, Suite B-232

Springfield, VA 22150-2311

(703) 451-0141

www.acanet.org

Preface

Paddling is a wonderful, diverse sport that appeals to a wide variety of Americans. Kayaking is the fastest-growing discipline within the sport of paddling, growing 272 percent from 1995 to 2003 according to outdoor recreation participation figures released by the Outdoor Industry Association. In fact, kayaking is *the* fastest growing outdoor sport. While sea kayaking and whitewater kayaking receive the bulk of media attention, most people enter the sport through what is known as "recreational kayaking."

Recreational paddlers enjoy paddling on easy rivers, less exposed coastal areas, lakes, ponds, and swamps. The rewards of recreational kayak touring are numerous, but while it is less risky than paddling on whitewater or serious sea kayaking, hazards do exist. Learning only from your mistakes can be a painful, even occasionally fatal, process, and there are much better ways of safely learning how to paddle. This book is intended to help the novice gain useful skills and knowledge, so that flatwater kayaking may be enjoyed in a safe, pleasurable manner.

The ideas and tips expressed here represent the collective wisdom of literally thousands of instructors who have tested and tried these techniques at thousands of paddling venues. We hope the information contained in this book will be as helpful to you as it has been to the many others who have gotten hooked on this beautiful, challenging sport.

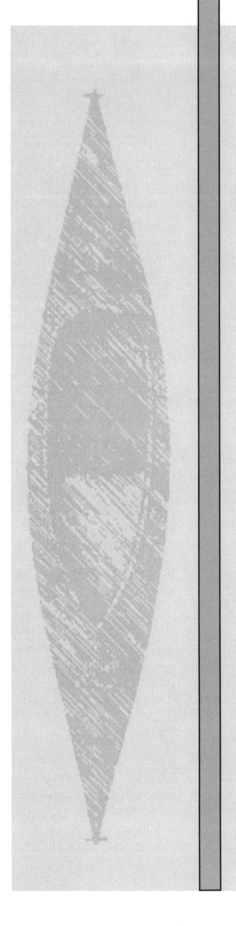

Introduction

Paddling safely requires, above all, the exercise of good judgment. And part of developing good judgment means understanding the various challenges and hazards inherent in any situation and one's own ability to meet them. To give an example, it is vital to know if a collision with another boat is imminent and how to avoid that collision. This book will help you gain the information and skills needed to make these kinds of all-important judgment calls. For instance, learning what kind of gear is appropriate for a given situation is a crucial part of paddling safely and effectively. This book, accordingly, opens with a chapter on selecting gear and on understanding how you can identify and manage risk. This book will guide you through the major facets of recreational kayaking on flatwater, including terminology, trip planning, stroke technique, safety and rescue, and much more. Each chapter contains detailed illustrations and photographs to help you better understand the concepts being presented. Furthermore, each section contains review questions designed to identify areas needing further study. The appendices contain other helpful information such as information on waterway security and a glossary of terms.

Ideally, this book should be considered part of an educational process that includes formal instruction. Lessons from a certified instructor are crucial for safety as well as for enjoyment. They will help you safely enjoy the sport and start you on the path to exercising good judgment while on the water. After completing your Essentials of Kayak Touring course with the ACA, join a local group of knowledgeable, experienced, sensible paddlers to increase your kayaking fun and safety.

Remember, too, that mastering one aspect of paddling, such as recreational kayaking, does not automatically launch you to the next level. Extreme venues such as whitewater and open-ocean conditions require specialized equipment and specialized skills. The transition from a gentle river to whitewater, or from a protected back bay to exposed open water can be difficult to recognize and unreasonably dangerous for recreational kayakers.

There is a wide spectrum of paddlers, ranging from those who enjoy still water to extreme paddlers who enjoy the most chaotic conditions imaginable. The goal for each paddler is to identify where on this spectrum he or she falls and then to learn and exercise the appropriate skills to be safe and have fun.

Gordon Black,

Director—Safety Education and Instruction

American Canoe Association

Other Resource Organizations

America Outdoors
(865) 558-3595
www.americaoutdoors.org

American Whitewater
(866) BOAT-4-AW
www.americanwhitewater.org

Professional Paddlesports Association
(703) 451-3864
www.propaddle.com

Trade Association of Paddlesports
(800) 755-5228
www.gopaddle.org

United States Canoe Association
(513) 422-3739
www.uscanoe.com

U.S.A. Canoe and Kayak
(704) 348-4330
www.usack.org

The following organizations provide general information on boating safety:

United States Coast Guard—Office of Boating Safety
www.uscgboating.org

United States Coast Guard Auxiliary
www.cgaux.org

National Association of State Boating Law Administrators
www.nasbla.org

National Safe Boating Council
www.safeboatingcouncil.org

United States Army Corps of Engineers
www.usace.army.mil

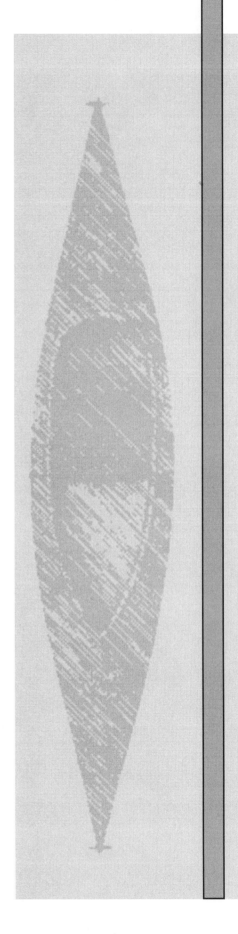

How to Be Safe on the Water

Rick is an avid fisherman. He has watched kayakers paddle into great fishing areas that larger boats can't access, so he decides to buy a kayak. At the big retail sports store he looks at the fancy paddling clothing, the exotic rescue gear, and the various paddles and life jackets. He decides to economize, so he figures he'll just wear his old jeans and a T-shirt, and since he knows he won't need to wear his life jacket (he was on his high school swim team), he thinks he can get away with the cheapest Type-IV cushion in the store.

The description above was compiled from actual accident reports. At the end of this chapter, you'll be given an opportunity to identify risk factors that Rick will likely encounter and to identify ways he can minimize or eliminate each risk.

Identifying and Reducing Risk

Become a safe paddler by reducing risk. Weather, water conditions, wind, temperature, equipment, prior planning, group composition, and experience all play a part in the safe-boating formula. Accepting your limitations, as well as those of your gear, and exercising good judgment will improve your chances of having a safe experience. Understanding the following key points will reduce your chances of a mishap and increase your enjoyment.

Using Crucial Equipment Appropriately

Life Jackets

According to the United States Coast Guard, most paddlers who drown are not wearing life jackets. The American Canoe Association requires that life jackets be worn during its paddling programs. Many states have similar requirements, and the United States Coast Guard requires everyone under the age of 13 to wear a properly sized and fitted life jacket while on a kayak. Life jackets provide buoyancy and work best when fitted securely. This means having zippers and buckles closed, and all adjustment straps "snugged" up. Make sure that the life jacket fits tightly enough around your torso that if you pull up on the shoulder straps the front of the jacket can't ride up above your chin. You should readjust and tighten your life jacket each time you put it on. Life jackets are also called personal flotation devices, or PFDs. Contact your state boating agency to learn about laws that require life jackets and other safety equipment to be carried on board a kayak. Be smart. Wear your life jacket.

Kayak Flotation

You need to wear a life jacket, and your boat needs extra flotation too. Even boats that are made of a buoyant material are difficult or impossible to rescue when full of water. Built-in waterproof

PFD

kayak float

compartments, foam blocks, or inflatable air bags are a must, and they must be securely attached to the boat. This extra flotation will help a swamped or capsized boat ride higher in the water, making rescue, emptying, and reentry much easier.

Clothing

Dress for the water temperature, not the air temperature. A layering system of clothing is important—air trapped between layers adds insulation. Adding or removing a layer of clothing allows easy comfort adjustment. Cotton clothing is a poor choice except in extreme heat, as cotton, once wet, holds moisture and cools the body. Wool and synthetic pile are much better insulators, wet or dry, but benefit from a windproof and waterproof outer layer to increase effectiveness. Proper insulation on head, hands, and feet increases paddler comfort in cold conditions. Extreme cold requires wet suits or synthetic insulation under dry suits. In addition to supplying crucial flotation, life jackets are also a valuable outside insulating layer.

Footwear

Footwear is a critical item of paddling gear. This is not the time to go barefoot! Cuts to the feet and sprained ankles are the most common injuries among inexperienced paddlers. Whether carrying a kayak over rugged, wet, and slippery terrain, or launching in ankle-deep water, choose good foot support and protection. In cold water, prudent paddlers should wear neoprene booties or old athletic shoes with wool or synthetic socks.

Additional Gear

What you carry will depend on your trip's length, access to supplies and services, and group make-up. For longer trips, consider taking the following: water bottle, sunglasses, sunscreen, insect repellent, first-aid kit, toilet paper, compass and maps, sponge, bailer (or better yet, a pump), whistle, flashlight, rescue rope and sling, knife, dry storage bags, extra paddle, matches, extra flotation for the kayak, duct tape, food, guidebooks, garbage bags, glasses straps, camera, fishing gear, and emergency signaling devices. Coast Guard regulations require anyone paddling on federally regulated water to carry a sounding device and a light. A bright flashlight and a loud whistle meet these requirements. Handheld aerosol horns are louder than whistles, and flares and signal mirrors can be helpful in some situations. Since conditions in ocean environments and on large lakes can deteriorate quickly, a prudent paddler may want to carry emergency communication devices. Cell phones work in many locations, but small two-way radios are much better. Cell phones won't contact the Coast Guard directly and won't allow you to contact other boats around you. VHF marine radios allow direct contact with the Coast Guard and other boats and can often pick up useful weather information. Carrying these in waterproof containers, and learning how to use them, can save your life! And a paddle float, discussed later, makes reentry after a flip much easier.

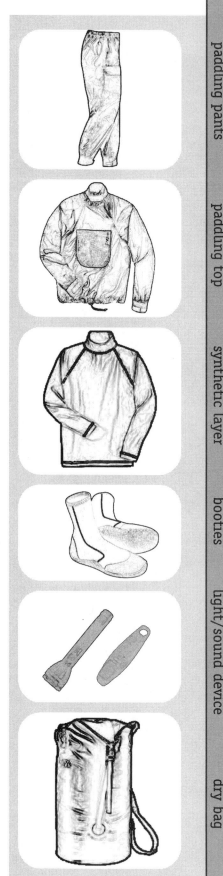

paddling pants

paddling top

synthetic layer

booties

light/sound device

dry bag

Preparing for Cold, Wind, and Waves
Hypothermia and Cold-Water Shock

Cold water can disable even the strongest of swimmers! Immersion in cold water (55° F or less) can cause immediate respiratory distress, cardiac arrest, and even loss of consciousness. Prolonged exposure to cold water can cause hypothermia, a condition that results in a lowering of your body's core temperature. Hypothermia develops when the body cannot produce enough heat to keep its temperature within a very narrow "normal" range. As your temperature drops, hypothermia sets in: unclear thinking, uncontrollable shivering followed by difficulty speaking, muscular rigidity, loss of coordination, and eventually loss of consciousness, then death.

Prevention is the key. The best way to prevent cold-water shock or hypothermia is to "Be Aware and Be Prepared!!" Wear proper clothing and a life jacket that fits. When the water temperature is 55° F or below, or when water and air temperatures combined don't add up to 120° F, wear a wet or dry suit and be sure to cover vulnerable areas such as your head, neck, and hands. Always carry extra dry clothes in a waterproof bag and consider bringing along a stove or thermos for hot drinks. Look for weather changes constantly. Be prepared and act quickly for yourself and those with you.

Wind and Waves

Wind produces waves on large bodies of water. Waves can be great fun, but can also lead to swamping or a capsized kayak. Stay in protected waters unless you and your group can handle rough water and are prepared to rescue overturned boats. Wind may either blow you off your intended course or slow your progress, and sometimes these setbacks can have serious consequences. Large waves are often found in flooded rivers, too. Floods are no place for the beginner, and recreational kayaks are not designed for such demanding conditions.

Learning Critical Skills
Wet Exits

Kayaks of all types do turn over, and you must be comfortable with exiting a capsized kayak. Sit-on-top kayaks and most inflatable kayaks are usually easy to exit , but a boat with decks, in which the paddler sits down, can present some challenges. A calm motion of bending forward at the waist, placing your hands on either side of the cockpit near your hips, and pushing the kayak toward your feet will allow you to safely exit even a tight cockpit. Leaning back while in the sitting position can make exiting much more difficult.

If a spray skirt (also called a spray deck) is used to keep water or rain out of the cockpit, you must practice removing the skirt and exiting the boat to ensure safety. Because many recreational kayaks have large cockpit openings, the skirts for those boats are quite large. Swimming with such a large amount of material around your

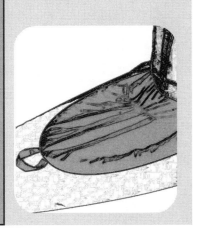

spray skirt

waist can be difficult, but should be practiced. Wet exits are best learned and practiced with an instructor standing beside the paddler to provide assistance and feedback. Spray skirts should not be used unless such practice has taken place.

Balance

You can decrease the chance of capsizing by staying low in the boat and being flexible at your waist. Let the boat rock back and forth, and maintain balance by keeping your head and torso over the centerline of the kayak. Sitting stiffly upright raises your center of balance, making capsize easier. Maintain a comfortably erect posture and let your hips swing with the boat's movement.

Understand the Paddling Environment

Open water on large lakes or at the ocean can be "glass smooth" or seething with foamy whitecaps. Smart paddlers understand that calm conditions can change in an instant. Fog challenges visibility and orientation. Learn to recognize and respect the dynamics of the water you are paddling. Experienced paddlers check weather forecasts, tide tables when paddling in tidal areas, and local information about how wind, waves, and currents work for or against the paddler in specific ways at specific sites. Up-to-date information helps paddlers determine where and when to paddle. This knowledge and planning opens the door to the fun and beauty of kayaking. The equipment, skills, and knowledge discussed in this book are only appropriate for protected areas in gentle conditions. Exercise good judgment! The thrills and rewards of venturing out into open water and rough conditions are many but require high-performance equipment, advanced skills, and the knowledge of how to meet these challenges safely. Don't let bad experiences form your judgment of paddling. Seek out more advanced instruction before you go after those thrills and rewards.

Review

From the scenario on page 1, list risk factors encountered by the kayaker.

1. _____

2. _____

3. _____

4. _____

5. _____

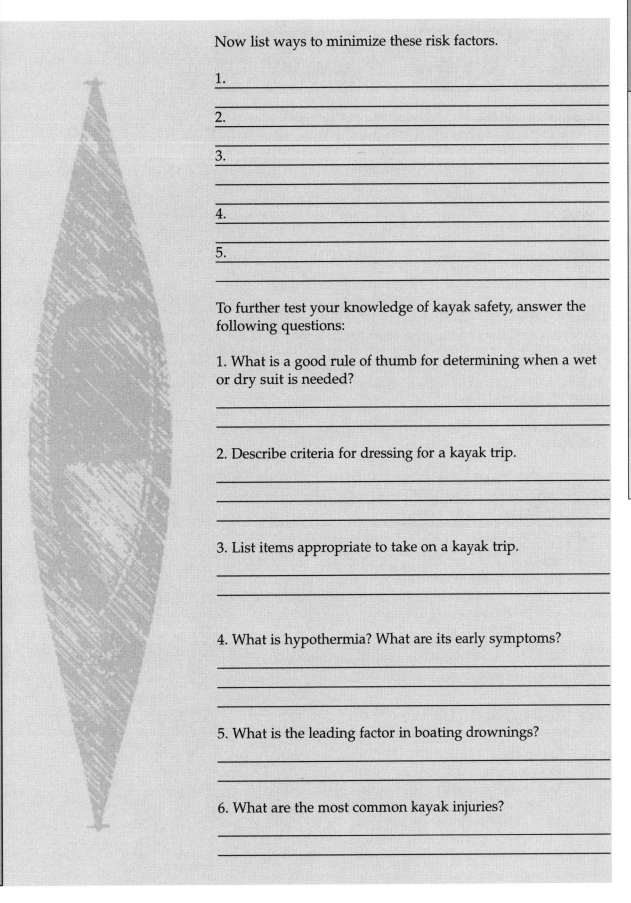

Now list ways to minimize these risk factors.

1. _____

2. _____

3. _____
   _____

4. _____

5. _____
   _____

To further test your knowledge of kayak safety, answer the following questions:

1. What is a good rule of thumb for determining when a wet or dry suit is needed?
_____
_____

2. Describe criteria for dressing for a kayak trip.
_____
_____
_____

3. List items appropriate to take on a kayak trip.
_____
_____

4. What is hypothermia? What are its early symptoms?
_____
_____
_____

5. What is the leading factor in boating drownings?
_____
_____

6. What are the most common kayak injuries?
_____
_____

Kayaks and Paddles

The store where Rick is shopping sells one kind of kayak. The salesperson assures Rick that it is perfect for fishing and offers to throw in a small pump for bilging out any water that splashes in. The boat's cockpit is large with plenty of room for Rick and his fishing gear, so he buys one.

Kayaks

There are a bewildering number of different kayak designs on the market. No single design will do everything well, so to refine your needs, you should determine how and where you expect to paddle. Taking ACA courses, seeking the opinions of experienced paddlers, and reading up on the sport (*Paddler* magazine is a great resource) are very good ways to gain information. Since there are so many different designs, not all descriptive terms apply to every boat. For instance, sit-on-top kayaks don't have cockpit rims, inflatables don't need supplemental flotation, and some boats do not have foot braces. The following section describes some design basics and introduces common terms.

Top View

1. **Stern.** The back portion of the kayak.
2. **Cockpit.** The opening in which you sit.
3. **Bow.** The front or forward part of the kayak.
4. **Deck.** The top of the kayak.
5. **Foot braces.** Pedals, walls, blocks, or ridges to rest your feet on. Often adjustable.
6. **Keel line.** A real or imaginary line from end to end down the center of the kayak.
7. **Seat.** Usually central if solo; if tandem, the bow seat is closer to the bow end.
8. **Backband.** A strap, pad, or foam block that supports the lower back.
9. **Cockpit rim.** Reinforced lip of the deck, surrounding the cockpit opening.

Side View (see facing page)

1. **Hull.** The body of the kayak.
2. **Cockpit rim.** Reinforced lip of the deck, surrounding the cockpit opening.
3. **Keel line.** The longitudinal centerline of the kayak.
4. **Backband.** A strap, pad, or foam block that supports the lower back. Also called the **coaming.**

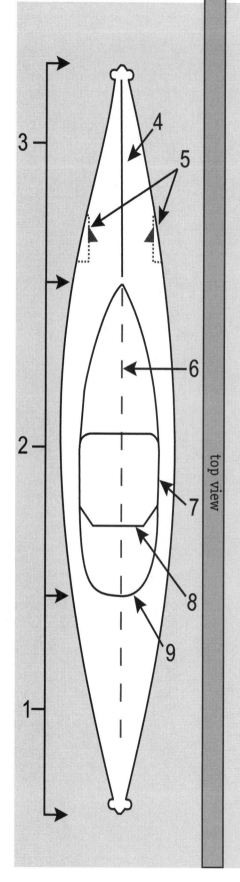

top view

Front View

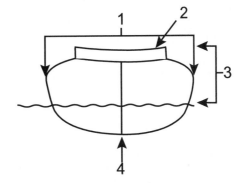

1. **Beam.** Width of the kayak at amidships.
2. **Cockpit rim.** Reinforced lip of the deck, surrounding the cockpit opening.
3. **Freeboard.** The vertical distance from the water surface to the lowest point along the side of the kayak.
4. **Keel line.** The longitudinal center line of the kayak.

Selecting a Kayak

Kayaks are made from many materials, including animal skin and bone, wood, wood and fabric, aluminum and fabric, fiberglass, sandwiched plastic, and plastic and fabric composites. Individual preferences regarding tradition, ruggedness, lightness, performance, and cost all influence the selection of construction material.

Length is an important kayak measurement—it plays a big part in determining maximum speed and helps indicate capacity. Longer kayaks are faster than shorter ones, but the increased drag of the longer surface area requires more energy to achieve a given speed.

Width and fullness give an indication of forward efficiency, seaworthiness, and ability to travel straight or "track." Narrow, fine-lined kayaks are efficient trackers, requiring less effort at given speeds than wider boats. Narrow kayaks track well but are not as stable as wider models.

Cross-sectional shaping affects stability. Flat-bottomed hulls have good initial stability but roll badly in waves. Rounder bottoms are less stable when entered but more stable in heavy seas and generally track well. Flared hulls maximize seaworthiness by deflecting waves outward but make vertical paddle strokes more difficult for smaller paddlers.

Rocker is the upturn of the hull along the keel line. It affects maneuverability and handling. More rocker allows a kayak to be turned easily. Less rocker increases tracking ability but reduces turning ability.

Select a kayak with **volume** appropriate to the weight to be carried. Remember that smaller kayaks are more efficient at moderate

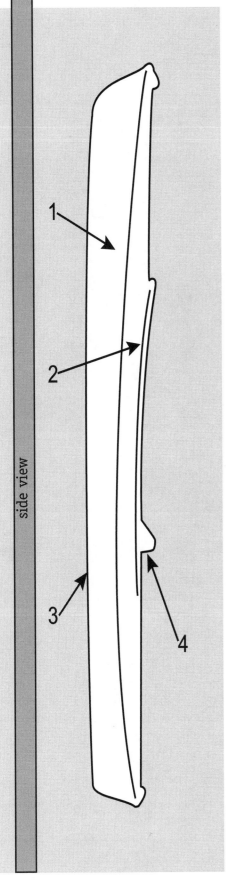

side view

speeds. Kayaks designed for touring or open ocean use tend to be long and lean with reduced rocker to enhance efficiency and tracking. Recreational kayaks usually have fuller lines (for stability) and more rocker (for maneuverability).

Paddles

The boat was less expensive than Rick had expected, so he decides to go for a really good paddle. He finds some exceptionally light short ones with bent shafts, and they come in sensational colors. When Rick realizes that these paddles cost more than the boat, he changes his mind and stays with his plan to be frugal. He buys the least expensive paddle in the store. It is short and light, with a thin aluminum shaft and soft rubber blades. The salesperson points out that the blades are unbreakable, no matter how much Rick bends them. Since the paddle is not quite as long as Rick is tall he figures it will be easy to handle.

The paddle transfers effort into kayak movement. Proper paddle size and style increases the boat's responsiveness and makes kayaking more fun. Just as boats come in a variety of sizes, shapes, and materials, selecting a paddle requires some choices. In general, a shorter paddle performs maneuvering strokes more quickly than a long paddle. Maneuvering is important for shorter boats in tight waterways. A longer paddle is better for straight-ahead touring, particularly in long boats. A taller paddler can more comfortably use a longer paddle than a shorter person can. At the end of a long day on the water a paddler, whether tall or short, will appreciate a light paddle.

Kayak Paddle

1. **Blade.** The flat section of the paddle which moves through the water.
2. **Tip.** The extreme end of each blade.
3. **Shaft.** The section of paddle between the blades.
4. **Throat.** The junction between blade and shaft.
5. **Powerface.** The side of the blade that catches the water during a forward stroke.
6. **Backface.** The other side of the blade.

Any length of paddle will probably work, but being comfortable and not having to compensate for a paddle that is too long or too short can make the difference between a difficult experience and an enjoyable outing. Using a long paddle in a tight stream can be frustrating, and having to frantically whip a short paddle back and forth to keep up with a group on open water is too much like work.

A 200-cm paddle (6 ft. 6.75 in.) is on the short end of the spectrum. A 240-cm paddle (7 ft. 10.5 in.) is on the long end. Longer and shorter paddles can be found if needed, but most paddlers choose a length in between 200 and 240 cm.

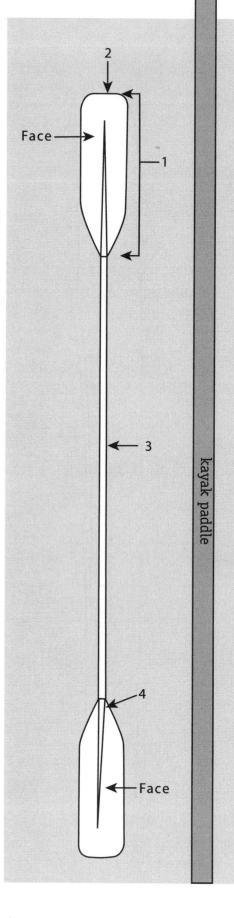

kayak paddle

Review

1. How do you measure for proper paddle length?

_____

_____

_____

2. How do you choose between shorter and longer paddles?

_____

_____

_____

3. Longer kayaks have the potential for greater _____ than shorter ones.

4. What is rocker and how does it affect a kayak's maneuverability?

_____

_____

_____

5. Describe the performance differences between kayaks with round versus flat bottoms.

_____

_____

_____

_____

Getting the Kayak into the Water

Rick puts the kayak in the back of his pick-up truck and drives down to a back bay area that he wants to fish. On the way to the water the boat starts to slip out of the back of Rick's truck, but he sees this before it can fall off the tailgate and stops. He uses some fishing line to tie the boat into the truck bed. When he finally reaches the boat launching area, he loads his fishing gear into the boat and carries it to the water. He flips the kayak a couple of times before he gets the hang of keeping his balance as he slides into the seat. Then he has trouble paddling off because one end of the boat is stuck on shore and, with his weight in the boat, he can't paddle out into deeper water. Finally, with much effort, he pulls free and heads out.

Tie Down

Kayaks should be secured amidships to cartop carriers (racks) and have both bow and stern tied to the vehicle's bumpers. Use two cross ropes or straps for the racks and tie two more ropes to the kayak ends; secure these ropes to bumpers or another solid part of your vehicle. Make sure the racks are secure and both the vehicle and racks are sturdy enough for the load. If you transport your kayak in a truck bed, be sure to tie it securely to the truck's attachment points so it can't slip out the back or blow away on the highway.

It is recommended that you use straps made of high-strength nylon webbing and strong buckles. If ropes are used, use proper knots such as the "truckers hitch," "half hitch," or "bowline." (See the ACA publication *Knots for Paddlers* for more information.)

Avoid the use of bungee or elastic cords. These may allow the boat to shift and fall off the car at highway speeds.

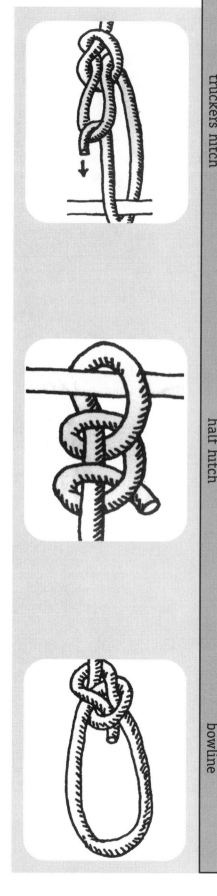

Lifting and Carrying the Kayak

Always lift a kayak using your legs to avoid back injury! Bend your knees to squat down beside the boat, roll the cockpit rim onto your shoulder, and straighten up carefully.

Lightweight solo kayaks can be carried short distances with the center point of the cockpit rim resting on a shoulder, the supporting arm grasping the rim just in front of the shoulder for control. Tandem boats, sit-on-tops, and heavier kayaks are carried more easily by two people. With a person on each end, kayaks can be carried by grasping beneath the boat's end or by holding the grab handles. Remember to bend your knees when putting the kayak down, and watch for unstable footing at the water's edge.

Launching the Kayak

Launching the kayak can be done many ways, depending on the shore. Different techniques can be helpful for docks, low banks, sandy beaches, etc. One easy method is to place the boat parallel to the shore in water that is deep enough to float the boat when loaded. In the shallows, the kayak is walked from shore into ankle-deep water. Always load cargo before paddlers. Trim the kayak level by equal load distribution.

Boarding the Kayak

To enter the kayak, lay the paddle across the boat behind the seat, with more paddle length toward shore. Facing forward, grasp the paddle with both hands behind you, and lean the kayak to shore until the paddle blade braces against the ground. Transfer your weight slowly onto the paddle and slide into the kayak's seat. The smaller the cockpit opening, the sooner you will have to bring your feet and legs into the front of the boat. In boats with very small cockpits you may have to sit on the deck behind the seat to put your legs in the boat first. Again, use the paddle to steady yourself. Maintain three points of contact when boarding and moving about in a kayak. Either two hands and one foot, or both feet and one hand should be in contact with the craft at all times. Climb directly into your paddling position whenever possible.

Balance and Stability

For maximum stability, stay loose! Imagine hinging your body at the waist. Keep your upper body and head over the centerline of the boat as you swing your hips from side to side. Start off by tipping the boat just a little back and forth, side to side. Staying flexible as the boat moves in the water is the key to maintaining balance. Most kayaks are very stable as long as you keep your balance.

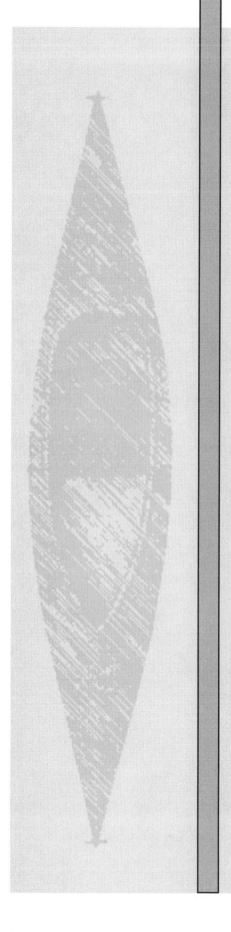

Leaning out over the side of the boat with your upper body is an easy way to turn over. Foot braces improve stability and paddling efficiency. Push against the foot brace on the same side as your paddle stroke to get the best energy transfer.

When paddling tandem, the stern paddler generally enters the kayak first. The stern paddler can then easily view the bow paddler's entry and help to steady the boat.

Review

1. Are bungee cords a good tool for securing your kayak to your vehicle? Why or why not?

_____

_____

_____

2. What muscles do the most work when picking up a kayak?

_____

_____

_____

_____

3. How can your paddle help you get into your kayak?

_____

_____

_____

_____

4. You should keep how many points of contact when moving about on a kayak?

_____

_____

_____

5. What is the best way to maintain balance once you are seated in the kayak?

_____

_____

_____

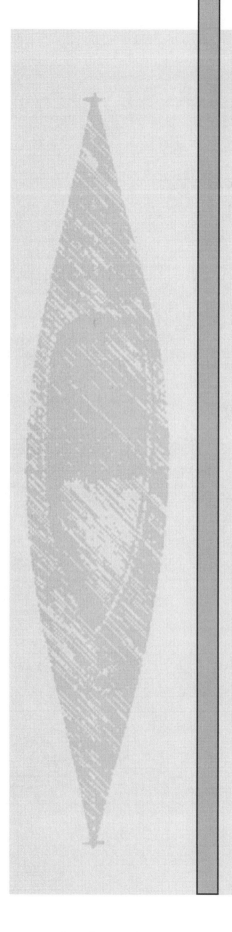

Kayaking Strokes

Paddling is the art of moving a kayak through the water. The key is to move your boat using maximum body and paddle efficiency. For best results, keep the paddle blade at right angles to the direction of travel; efficiency fades quickly as the angle changes. Keep the shaft vertical to the water surface when moving forward or in reverse. Keep the shaft horizontal on sweep strokes, which are used to turn the boat. Perfectly vertical forward strokes are efficient, but can be tiring. It's fine to relax, lower your hands a bit, and let the paddle shaft become more horizontal. Just remember that if you need to hurry a more vertical stroke will generally move you more quickly.

Holding the Paddle

When holding the paddle, space your hands apart a bit more than shoulder width. Maintain a relaxed grip, don't squeeze the shaft too tightly. Sit up straight but twist your torso to reach as far forward as possible. As you move the boat by pulling your paddle against the water, use the large torso muscles to power the kayak. Your arms help with the stroke, but if you rely on just your arms you will tire more quickly.

Paddle Stroke Phases

Paddle strokes have three phases: catch, propulsion, and recovery. The paddle enters the water during the catch at right angles to the direction of travel or resistance. During the propulsion phase the kayak moves in a given direction. Recovery with a kayak paddle often means simply reaching forward with the other blade to start

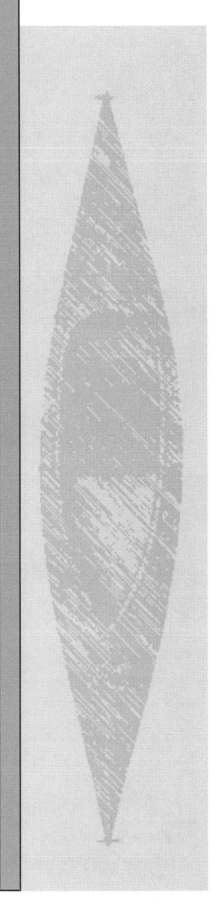

another catch. As the new blade moves into position for a catch, the first one comes up out of the water. Sometimes, as with sweeps or ruddering, successive strokes may be taken on the same side, with the same blade. In this case the working blade is "recovered" to the starting position for repeating the stroke.

Stroke Terminology

Understanding the following terms will make the stroke descriptions more useful. Review the Glossary of Terms on pages 37–39 for more terms.

Working blade   The blade that is in the water, applying force.

Offset   This refers to the two blades of a kayak paddle not being in the same plane. Various offsets are used for different purposes. Having offset blades can reduce resistance on the nonworking blade as it moves through the air toward the next stroke. No offset, where the two blades line up with each other, is the simplest design (see p. 8).

Control hand   A paddle with offset blades needs to be twisted between each stroke so that each catch can take place with the blade at 90 degrees to the direction of travel. This angle allows the blade to achieve the greatest possible resistance and increases efficiency. Only one hand is used to control this twisting; otherwise the paddler's wrists may be uncomfortable or even injured. Most modern paddles are right-hand controlled, which means the paddle shaft is held firmly by the right hand and twisted by that hand when necessary. The left hand loosely holds the shaft, allowing it to rotate as needed. This loose grip is very important for avoiding wrist injury. In fact, a relaxed grip with both hands is safer and much less fatiguing. Left-hand-control paddles are available but can be hard to find.

Indexed grip   So that the paddler can orient the paddle blades without looking at them, the grip area on the shaft is an oval shape, or "indexed," designed to fit into the palm of your control hand. Some paddles don't have this feature, especially ones without offset blades.

The Strokes

While paddling strokes may be modified or combined to achieve the movement or reaction desired of the kayak, it is helpful to have a kayak paddle in your hands as you read the stroke descriptions that follow. All strokes can be practiced while sitting in a straight-backed chair.

The photos on pages 16–18 show solo paddlers, but all of the strokes can be adapted for tandem kayaking.

Because kayaks tend to turn under power, we first present turning and spinning strokes. These include various draws and sweeps.

Learning these strokes first will allow you to turn at will, and to stop turning at will, so you will be able to control your craft. Forward and reverse strokes are presented last.

Draw

The draw moves the kayak abeam (sideways) toward the paddle, or can turn the kayak when used at either end. The draw begins as the paddler twists to one side, aligning his or her shoulders with the centerline of the boat. The catch begins off the paddler's hip, with both arms extended and the paddle as vertical as possible. The blade is parallel to the keel line, the powerface toward the kayak.

The draw is powered by pulling the onside hip toward the paddle, keeping the top arm stiff and bending the bottom arm slightly. As the kayak approaches the blade the power phase of the draw stroke ends. To recover, rotate the working blade so that you can slice the edge of the blade through the water to the catch position. Rotate the working blade back in line with the keel line to begin the next draw. This is an "in-water recovery."

Keep the paddle vertical in the water to increase efficiency.

Hint: Moving the boat to the paddle creates the illusion of trying to pull water under the kayak. Think of your paddle as a broom that you are using to sweep dirt under a carpet!

Ruddering

Drawing in or pushing away with the paddle blade behind the paddler near the stern is called "ruddering" and is a useful steering technique once you have forward momentum. Body position is the same as for the draw, with the shoulders as nearly in line with the keel line as possible. The paddle is held fairly horizontally, with the working blade planted back near the stern, and on edge. With the blade fully immersed, push away or pull in toward the stern to steer. Keep the rearmost arm's elbow low, near the back deck. This will put less strain on the shoulder joint.

Bow Draw

Draws to the bow, or "bow draws," are quite useful in certain situations, such as turning across eddy lines (see Glossary of Terms). Start in the same body position as for the draw, but with the paddle held on an angle with the working blade planted well forward and about two or three feet from the bow. Pull the bow toward the paddle, again using the torso muscles to power the stroke.

Sculling Draw

Sculling is easier to do than to describe. Start as with a draw, with the paddle beside you. Slice the paddle through the water, first toward the bow, then back toward the stern. In which ever direction the paddle is moving make sure the "leading edge" of the blade is cocked slightly away from the boat. The paddle blade never lifts out of the water, and the boat will move abeam. This is an easy, graceful

draw

ruddering

bow draw

sculling draw

stroke, good for maneuvering, and for impressing friends. As with any stroke, practice before showing off.

Forward Sweep

The forward sweep (also called simply "a sweep") turns the bow away from the working blade while maintaining forward momentum. The paddle shaft is held horizontally during the forward sweep. The paddler leans forward slightly, rotating the torso 45 degrees toward the direction the boat is to turn (the working blade's arm and shoulder reaches forward). At the catch, the paddle blade is on edge in the water alongside the bow. Using torso rotation to power the stroke, arc the blade in a wide semicircle to the stern. Watch the paddle blade as it moves through the semicircle to help generate torso motion. Extend both arms to arc the paddle out as far away from the boat as possible without compromising balance, with both hands eventually out over the water. The rearmost arm should bend slightly only as the blade nears the stern. Bending the arm at this point is important to protect the shoulder from potential injury. If another sweep is needed, return the paddle from the stroke's end to the catch position and repeat.

Reverse Sweep

The reverse sweep turns the kayak sharply toward the working blade, reducing forward momentum.

The paddler's body rotates toward the direction you want the boat to turn, with the working blade planted close beside the stern, and on edge. The paddle shaft is held horizontally. The arm closest to the stern is slightly bent (elbow down) with the hand well behind the paddler's hip. With the paddler looking at the blade, the torso uncoils, arcing the blade out from the boat and forward, and pushing the blade's backface against the water. The bow swings toward the stroke with the stern swinging away. Recover by twisting back to the plant position if another reverse sweep is needed. The solo paddler's sweep arcs 180 degrees and travels from "tip to tip," or end to end, of the kayak. In a tandem kayak the team performs sweeps together, on the same side of the boat. Care and communication are needed to keep from banging paddles, but nearly full sweep strokes are still possible.

Forward Stroke

The forward stroke moves the kayak forward and is the key to successful paddling. A stroke on one side of the boat will turn the boat away from that stroke. The farther out the paddle arcs away from the boat, the more the boat will turn. Alternating strokes from side to side will correct that veer, but for increased efficiency keep the forward stroke parallel to the keel line, as close to the boat as possible, and relatively short to keep the blade vertical through the power phase.

Reach as far forward as you can without leaning and then twist your torso to reach even farther. Twisting allows you to use large muscle groups in your torso, and leaning forward prevents effective twisting. Plant the paddle so that the entire blade is in the water. Allow your torso to "untwist" back to a neutral position, using those torso muscles along with your arm to pull against the paddle. Imagine pulling the boat forward past the paddle, remembering to keep the blade as close as possible to the boat. Lift the working blade out of the water when it is near your hip and reach forward with the other blade for the next stroke. Taking the stroke farther back wastes energy by lifting water and turning the kayak.

Back Stroke

The back stroke is used to stop forward motion or to move the kayak backwards.

This stroke is simply the forward stroke done in reverse. Slice the blade into the water near your hip and push it forward until it comes out of the water near your bow. Keep the blade close to the boat and alternate sides as you would with a forward stroke. Twisting your torso into this stroke will give you more power, but since most folks find backing up quite challenging, more power may not be a good idea. This stroke (done slowly with correct form) is good for warming up shoulder muscles, and frequent practice will really improve your overall boat control.

Maneuvers

When you perform a stroke, it seems that the paddle is moving relative to you and the boat. Of course, the object is for the boat to move. The movements of the boat on the water, including spins, turns, moving abeam, and many more, are called maneuvers. A few very simple maneuvers include:

Spins

Spins rotate the boat on its center. Solo kayaks spin easily with sweeps or reverse sweeps. Tandem kayaks can spin with several

Working Blade ➡

Working Blade ➡

mixtures of bow and stern strokes. In tandem boats with seating positions close to each other, you must take care not to whack your partner with the paddle on these combined strokes. The two working blades will be on opposite sides of the boat, and the nonworking end of the paddle can get in the way.

Turns

To turn the kayak while moving, select strokes that reduce drag. While a variety of strokes may turn the kayak, the following strokes are most effective at maintaining forward momentum:

➤ Turn solo kayaks using a draw stroke to the bow, or a sweep.
➤ Turn tandem kayaks by combining a bow draw with a stern sweep.

Moving Sideways (Abeam)

This maneuver moves the kayak sideways without turning it. Moving abeam is useful for leaving and approaching shore and avoiding obstacles in tight passages. Draws and pushaways move the boat abeam. Pushaways are particularly useful when bringing a boat to shore or to a dock. As the kayak gets close to shore, there may not be enough distance or depth to properly perform a draw, so a pushaway on the side away from shore is the stroke of choice.

Paddling a Double or "Tandem" Kayak

Tandem paddlers work together as a team. The bow paddler sets the cadence; the stern paddler reads and follows the bow's lead. The bow, however, should feel the rhythm of strokes and listen for instructions from the stern. Bow and stern usually paddle on the same side of the boat, in unison. This keeps the paddles from banging into each other and lessens the chance of one paddler accidentally hitting the other. Remember, it takes time, patience, and lots of communication to build a tandem team.

Review

1. What is the proper hand positioning on the paddle?

_____

_____

_____

_____

2. Why are feathered recoveries important? (see the Glossary of Terms for help with this one)

_____

_____

_____

_____

3. Name three key points about tandem paddling.

_____

_____

_____

_____

_____

4. Why should you keep the paddle shaft vertical on draws, pushaways, forward, and backstrokes?

_____

_____

_____

_____

5. Why should you hold the shaft nearly horizontal for sweeps and reverse sweeps?

_____

_____

_____

_____

6. What phase of the paddle stroke transfers the most force to the water?

_____

_____

_____

_____

7. Name the three parts of a stroke.

_____

_____

_____

_____

8. How should the paddle shaft be oriented during a sweep stroke?

_____

_____

_____

9. a. Where should the paddle blade be at the start of the forward stroke?

_____

_____

b. How far back should the blade move during the forward stroke?

_____

_____

_____

10. How do you keep from slowing down while turning?

_____

_____

_____

11. When might you want to move the kayak abeam?

_____

_____

_____

12. How can tandem kayakers avoid hitting each other's paddles?

_____

_____

_____

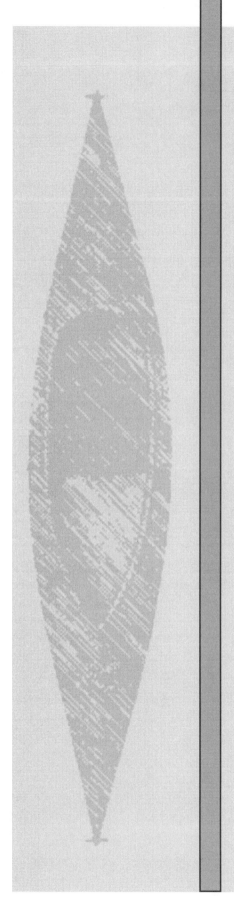

Kayak Touring

Rick finds the kayak is easy to paddle and heads for a shallow tidal area that he has been wanting to fish. To get to that area he must cross a busy channel, with boats and barges moving much faster than he can paddle. He waits for a gap between boats and tries to sprint across the channel, but misjudges the speed of a commercial tugboat that is pushing a number of barges. Rick finds himself in front of the oncoming "tow" and barely gets out of the path of the deceptively fast-moving barge. As the tug moves past, a turbulent wake tosses Rick's kayak enough that he loses his balance, and he finds himself swimming!

Paddling on lakes, protected coastal areas, and other flatwater sites can be rewarding and enjoyable. To make sure your experience is a safe one remember that hazards do exist. Safe environments can become dangerous quickly. Fog, bad weather, sea conditions, and other dangers can suddenly put you at serious risk. Learn to recognize hazards and avoid them before an emergency happens. Prepare yourself by checking expected weather conditions, study maps and charts of the area in which you will be paddling, and always paddle with a group. Leave information about your intended trip (a float plan) with family, friends, or authorities.

A natural tendency for paddlers who have enjoyed some easy paddling is to go on more challenging trips. This too can be very rewarding, but skills and knowledge must be increased progressively if the paddler is to maintain personal safety.

For instance, strokes and maneuvers executed and developed on flatwater provide an excellent foundation for paddling on moving water. In addition to basic strokes, you need to understand current dynamics and how to "read" the current. You also should understand the force of moving water. A gallon of water weighs about

eight pounds. The faster water flows, the greater kinetic energy, or force, it creates. Hundreds, even thousands, of pounds of force can be created against a pinned person or boat.

By understanding the characteristics of the moving-water environment, you can develop respect for that environment. Take an ACA river paddling course to learn more about moving water before venturing out onto rivers.

The paddler should be aware that some of the hazards found on rivers can be present on flatwater too. This is because large bodies of water often have currents present, and to make matters more complicated, tidal action can cause some of these currents to change direction. Large rapids can form in narrow passages as tidal currents reach peak velocities. Wind can also cause problems, such as large waves on flatwater. And a pier or dock can form a dangerous strainer as current pushes against its supports. Current will form eddies behind any obstruction, such as bridge piers, small islands, peninsulas jutting into channels, and even behind moving ships. The current differential (eddy line) can be extremely powerful and capable of twisting a kayak out of control or even capsizing it. Strong wind, current, tidal action, and boat traffic can all be safely dealt with, but only by well-trained, experienced, properly equipped paddlers. Seek out instruction and supportive groups of experienced paddlers if you want to explore areas where these forces and phenomena are present. Otherwise stay in protected waters, away from high traffic or areas subject to the forces of open water. Remember that you determine how much risk you'll expose yourself to. Don't *let* bad things happen; *make* safety a priority. Make sure you are trained, prepared, and equipped for the activity and location you are exploring.

Rules of the Road

Practically every other boat you encounter while paddling, unless it is another kayak, will be bigger and faster than you are. Captains of these craft find it difficult to see a kayaker because kayaks are low in the water and typically leave little or no wake. Self-preservation dictates that the kayaker must be constantly on the lookout, ready to avoid traffic.

Regulations published by the United States Coast Guard determine how all vessels on all waterways interact. Known as "Rules of the Road," these can be found on the Coast Guard's Web site, www.uscg.mil. Go to "Our Missions"—"Maritime Mobility"—"Rules of the Road." You should be familiar with and understand these rules, but you should also realize that small and fast recreational boats may not see you, and larger ships may not be able to stop fast enough, maneuver around you, or see you. The responsibility for avoiding collisions and near misses is ultimately yours. You can make yourself more visible by wearing bright, high-visibility colors or attaching bright 360-degree-visible white lights to yourself in low-light situations. You can also improve your radar "signature" by using special materials and paints on your paddle and other gear, but again, your best bet for avoiding collisions is constant vigilance.

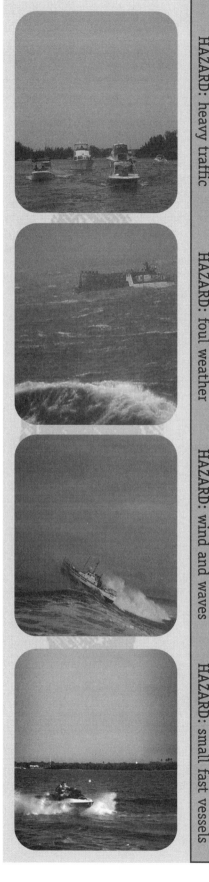

The basic rule is to do whatever is necessary to avoid collision. Of course, part of avoiding a collision means knowing when one could occur. On open water, where other boats are sometimes visible, use the bow-angle method to determine whether you and another craft are on a collision course. To do this, point your arm or paddle at the other craft. Monitor the angle formed between your bow and a straight line pointed at the other craft. If the angle is reducing, the craft will pass in front of you. If the angle is increasing, the craft will pass behind you. But if it remains constant, you are on a collision course and should alter your course. Remember that the other boat may alter course. Some shipping lanes, for example, have established turning points, so the distant freighter on a course to cross your bow may, in a few minutes time, be heading right at you. Constantly sweep the horizon around you and recheck the position of other craft using the bow-angle method.

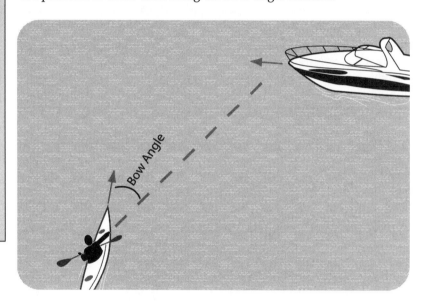

Remember that distances can be deceptive on open water and that large commercial boats are often moving much faster than they appear. When dealing with large commercial vessels, you should assume that you are invisible to them and take steps to simply stay out of their way. These large craft are less maneuverable than you and can take literally miles to stop, so just because the pilot sees you doesn't mean he or she can avoid you. It helps to know ahead of time where you are likely to encounter ships and large commercial craft. Check marine charts or maps ahead of time for designated shipping lanes, but remember that commercial boats (such as large fishing boats) can also be found in other waters.

When encountering smaller craft like powerboats, personal watercraft such as jet-powered skis, and sailboats, know the Rules of the Road and exercise good judgment. In general, you should always be prepared to give way since you are more likely to suffer from a collision. When sharing a channel with larger boats paddle close to the edge of the channel, preferably close to shore. The larger boat may not have enough depth to safely pass you otherwise. In all open-water situations, you should act predictably. If a larger faster

KAYAK TOURING

boat proceeds to pass near you, you should maintain course and speed. When encountering another vessel, if you must change course, do so in a clear and deliberate fashion so that your new trajectory will be as obvious as possible to the other boat operator. The bow-angle method works as well with smaller craft as with large ships, but remember that these smaller boats are more likely to alter course frequently. When you get closer, try to make eye contact with the operator, since this an excellent way to make sure he or she knows you are there.

Departure Checklist

➤ Communication plan
➤ Travelling patterns: stay together, lead and sweep boats
➤ Weather forecast
➤ Route for the day
➤ Rendezvous point in case of separation
➤ Local hazards (rip tides, currents, winds, etc.)
➤ Legal safety and lighting requirements for boating for the area you will be in
➤ Float or paddle plan filed with local authorities and friends that includes:

Planned route

Number in party

Description of boats

Expected return, time/day

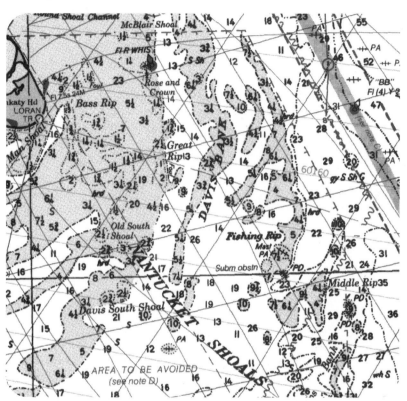

Navigation charts such as this indicate shipping channels, water depth, and many other features. The wide, shaded line on this navigation chart indicates a shipping channel.

Remember too that weather and water conditions will affect how other boats respond to you. For example, in situations where there is a strong current, powerboats will be better able to avoid you than will sailboats under sail. Significant waves may make it even harder for other boats to see you, and such waves and current may compromise your ability to get out of the way. Always be alert—maintain an acute sense of what is happening around you at all times and think ahead about how you might respond.

The most important step you can take to improve your safety and knowledge about kayaking is to take an ACA kayaking course. Definitive information on the "Rules of the Road" can be found at the United States Coast Guard Web site, www.uscg.mil. One of the most valuable books for kayakers who venture out on the ocean and other large bodies of open water is John Lull's *Sea Kayaking Safety & Rescue* (Wilderness Press, 2001), and much of the material in this section is based on his chapter "Dealing with Boat Traffic." Lull summarizes how to avoid a collision with boat traffic as follows:

➤ Use a chart to identify shipping lanes; know when you are in shipping lanes, and paddle in them only as necessary.
➤ Familiarize yourself with the "Rules of the Road," especially where they apply to kayaks and other small craft.
➤ Stay alert and maintain a constant watch in all directions for other vessels.
➤ Learn and use the bow-angle method of detecting possible collision.
➤ Make yourself as visible as possible.
➤ Act in a predictable way; stay close together when paddling in a group.
➤ Know what the current is doing and how it affects you and other craft.
➤ Always carry a bright light when paddling at night.
➤ Adjust your collision-avoidance strategy for different types of watercraft.

Review

1. What is a float plan?

_____

_____

2. Where can you find the "Rules of the Road"?

_____

3. What is the bow-angle method?

_____

_____

4. Name a hazard involving large vessels other than collision.

_____

_____

5. Besides a PFD what safety equipment items does the Coast Guard require kayakers to carry?

_____

_____

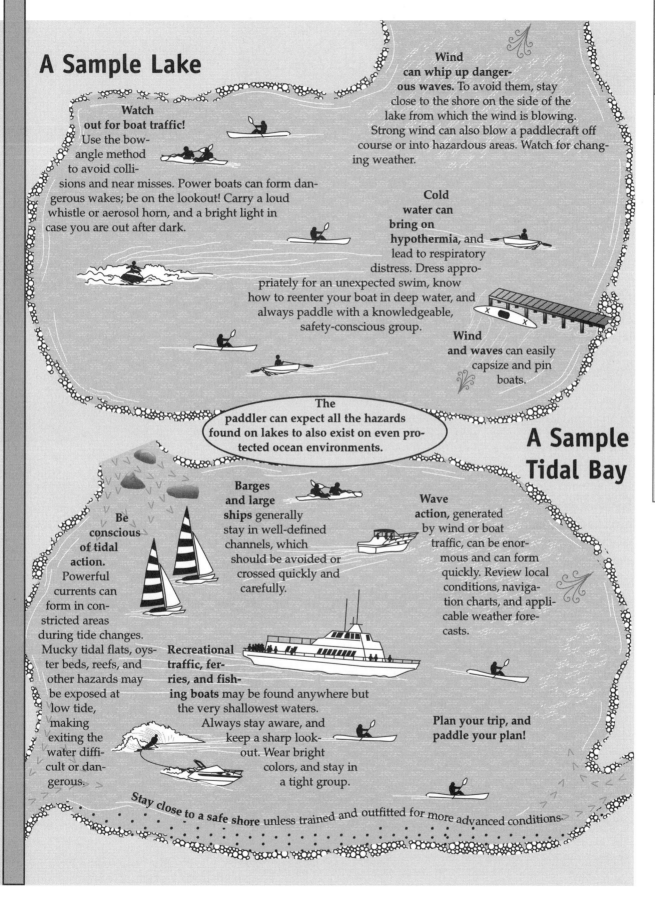

A Sample Lake

Watch out for boat traffic! Use the bow-angle method to avoid collisions and near misses. Power boats can form dangerous wakes; be on the lookout! Carry a loud whistle or aerosol horn, and a bright light in case you are out after dark.

Wind can whip up dangerous waves. To avoid them, stay close to the shore on the side of the lake from which the wind is blowing. Strong wind can also blow a paddlecraft off course or into hazardous areas. Watch for changing weather.

Cold water can bring on hypothermia, and lead to respiratory distress. Dress appropriately for an unexpected swim, know how to reenter your boat in deep water, and always paddle with a knowledgeable, safety-conscious group.

Wind and waves can easily capsize and pin boats.

The paddler can expect all the hazards found on lakes to also exist on even protected ocean environments.

A Sample Tidal Bay

Be conscious of tidal action. Powerful currents can form in constricted areas during tide changes. Mucky tidal flats, oyster beds, reefs, and other hazards may be exposed at low tide, making exiting the water difficult or dangerous.

Barges and large ships generally stay in well-defined channels, which should be avoided or crossed quickly and carefully.

Wave action, generated by wind or boat traffic, can be enormous and can form quickly. Review local conditions, navigation charts, and applicable weather forecasts.

Recreational traffic, ferries, and fishing boats may be found anywhere but the very shallowest waters. Always stay aware, and keep a sharp lookout. Wear bright colors, and stay in a tight group.

Plan your trip, and paddle your plan!

Stay close to a safe shore unless trained and outfitted for more advanced conditions.

Rescue and Safety

Rick isn't wearing a life jacket when his boat flips over, but he was sitting on the Type IV seat cushion/life preserver in his kayak. He looks around for his boat but sees nothing in all the chop and waves kicked up by passing boats. He occasionally catches sight of his seat cushion floating, but it is being blown away from him pretty fast. And the passing boats are moving fast also, too fast to see Rick in the water. He starts swimming toward shore. Finally one boater does see him and stops to help. After Rick is helped onboard, the boat's captain heads over to the floating life preserver and picks it up, but there is no sign of the kayak.

Rescue

Capsizing is part of the sport of paddling. Boaters should be able to handle their own craft in capsizes or swamps and aid others in need. Whether assisting others or saving yourself, remember that people come first! You may need to let go of a boat or other gear if you are being swept toward a hazard. Always be prepared to swim. Dress properly and wear your life jacket. Remember, any rescue will be safer and easier if the boat has adequate flotation. This means having inflated air bags, foam blocks, or waterproof compartments in the boat. Without this supplemental flotation some boats may be impossible to rescue. Being prepared is the first step in a rescue.

Self-Rescue

Self-rescue is often the quickest and surest way to deal with capsizing. The simplest self-rescue is to wade or swim to the closest safe shore with the kayak. On flatwater, if the self-rescue involves a long

swim, you may want to reenter the boat even if it is partially flooded. With an assisting paddler stabilizing the swamped boat, scrambling on and into your boat is quite possible, or you can use a paddle float to stabilize the swamped boat yourself. Whatever method you rely on will require practice in controlled conditions if you want it to work in an emergency. Whenever possible, stay with the boat even if you can't reenter the craft. It provides positive flotation, and a large object is more visible to rescuers as well as to powerboats that might otherwise not see you. Remember! You must have supplemental flotation, securely attached to the boat, so the boat will ride high even when full of water. Air bags and waterproof compartments must be inspected prior to each trip to make sure they are functioning properly.

Emptying the Kayak

To empty a capsized boat floating in shallow water where you can stand near shore, turn the boat so that it points toward the shore. Push down on the end of the boat that is away from shore and push the other end up onto the land. With the kayak still upside down, raise the end that is away from shore so that the water drains out. A kayak full of water is very heavy, so keep your knees bent, back straight, and get help, if possible, to avoid back injury. After allowing several seconds for the boat to drain, roll the kayak to the upright position on the surface of the water. In deeper water, a boat-over-boat rescue is most effective (see p. 32).

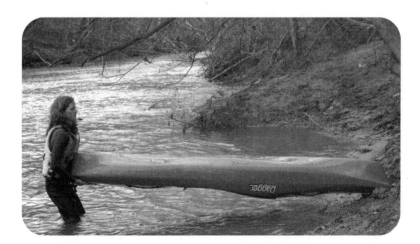

Reentering the Kayak in Deep Water

If shore access is not possible, you can reenter the kayak from deep water. One method is to crawl up on top of the boat from the stern with your legs straddling the boat. Bring your legs forward and slide into the seat when you reach it. If your boat is very wide (beamy) you can enter from the side. Begin by placing your hands on both sides of the cockpit rim near the wide section of the kayak, although hand placement may vary due to kayak width and stability, arm length, and paddler strength. There should be space available for your body inside the open cockpit. Pressing down with both hands and using a strong kick, lift the body upwards until the hips are across the near side. If the cockpit is large enough roll onto your back and sit inside the kayak before bringing in your legs.

Balancing the boat during these maneuvers is difficult and requires practice. A second boat can assist by holding the cockpit rim or side opposite the side being reentered, stabilizing the boat. Tandem paddlers help stabilize the boat for their partners and reenter one at a time. Accessories such as paddle floats, sponsons, or a rescue sling can help you get back in your boat, but no matter the technique or gear you rely on, practice is key.

After reentry, hand-paddle the boat, if necessary, to retrieve paddles and gear. Swamped kayaks may be paddled to shore with paddles, or if necessary with your hands. They may also be bailed or pumped dry. Carrying a bail bucket or pump is an important part of being properly prepared.

Rescuing Others

In order to minimize risk to themselves rescuers should use the least dangerous technique to affect a rescue. When in position to assist others, use this rescue sequence: Reach—Throw—Row—Go (see facing page). These techniques are progressively more dangerous to the rescuer. Training, practice, and preparation are necessary prerequisites of rescuing yourself and others.

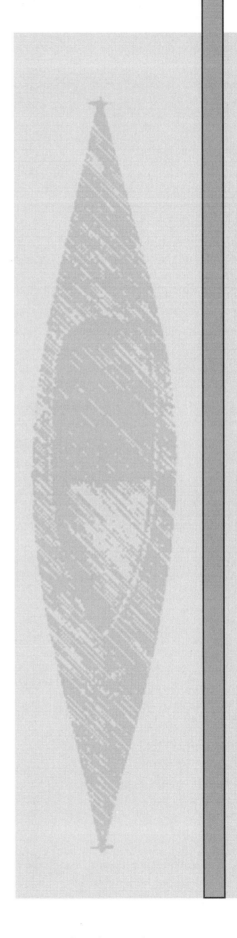

Reach—Throw—Row—Go

Reach

First reach with your voice. A call or a whistle blast to get the victim's attention is a good idea. Often, reaching a hand to a swimming paddler can bring him or her safely to shore or to your boat. A paddle can extend your reach safely.

Throw

When the swimmer is too far away to reach with a paddle or pole, a thrown float or rope can often aid in the paddler's rescue.

Row

If the swimmer is beyond range of a thrown rescue device, the rescuer should maneuver his or her boat closer so that a reach or throw technique is possible. A rescuer in a boat is safer than a swimming one.

Go

As a last option, a trained and properly equipped rescuer can swim to the aid of the swimmer. Bystanders should call for help.

Bulldozer Rescue

When rescuing a swimmer, tow the swimmer at the stern of your kayak while bumping (bulldozing) the swamped boat to calm water at a close shore. Instruct the swimmer to kick her legs to help out, as bulldozing is hard work.

Boat-over-Boat Rescue

In open water with a second kayak to assist as a rescue boat, a boat-over-boat rescue is quick and very effective. Assume a kayak has capsized:

The capsized boater helps line the capsized boat up perpendicular to the rescue boat forming a **T**, and remains in the position at the bottom of the **T**. The rescuer at the top of the **T** holds onto the capsized boat's end, allowing the capsized boater to push down on the away end of the boat, raising the near end up and out of the water. Keeping the boat upside down, the rescuer pulls the boat up and across their craft until it balances on their boat forming a **+**. Be careful not to pinch fingers between the two boats. The capsized paddler should keep hold of the upside-down kayak as it is pulled up and over, then move to a stabilizing position on the end of the rescue boat. The rescuer allows the boat to drain, then flips it upright while continuing to balance it across their own boat. The rescuer slides the kayak into the water without losing contact. The two boats are then held side to side while the swimmer reenters the boat.

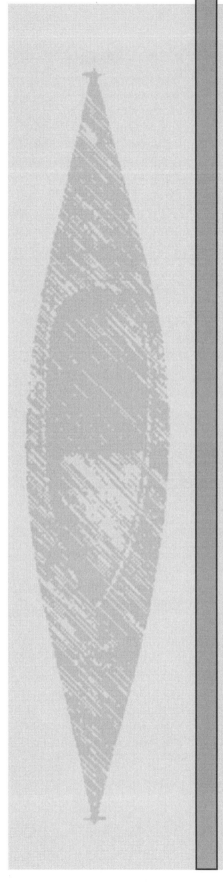

Remember that any of these techniques may be impossible unless the boat is equipped with supplemental flotation. Whatever type—air bags, foam, or watertight compartments—added flotation should be inspected and maintained regularly.

Rescue Sling

A rescue sling enables a swimmer to more easily reenter a boat. Loop over the side of the swimmer's boat a section of line or webbing long enough to hang into the water. Place the loop across the boat onto a second boat or onto a paddle placed crossways beneath both boats. If a second paddler is in the water to help stabilize, secure the loop directly around the cockpit rim or around the hull of the boat being entered. The paddler then places a foot in the loop, using it like a stirrup. Lifting the hips above the top of the cockpit, the paddler climbs into the center of the boat.

Exposure in Water

When paddlers are unable to reenter their craft quickly, they may risk hypothermia, especially if water or air temperature is low. The Heat Escape Lessening Posture (HELP) and HUDDLE position minimize heat loss in cold water.

The HELP Position

The HELP position protects the highest heat-loss areas of the body: the head, neck, underarms, and groin area. This technique is possible only when wearing a life jacket. To adopt the HELP position, the individual swimmer:

➤ Crosses the legs at the ankles and pulls the legs toward the chest.
➤ Crosses the arms at the chest being careful to protect the area under the arms, or holds the neck with the hands for additional protection.
➤ Keeps the head out of the water.

The Huddle

A group of paddlers huddling together conserves body temperature more efficiently than floating alone. To HUDDLE, body-to-body contact is critical. Form a circle, placing smaller or weaker individuals inside. Wrap arms around one another with legs together.

Review

1. Name the steps in the rescue sequence.

_____

_____

2. Why stay with the kayak when capsized or swamped?

_____

_____

3. Name two methods for emptying a swamped kayak.

_____

_____

4. Describe two techniques for minimizing heat loss in cold water.

_____

_____

5. What could Rick have done differently to make swimming easier and safer?

_____

_____

6. What could Rick have done to prevent the loss of his kayak?

_____

Appendices

Waterway Security

Because of Homeland Security concerns, many Federal properties now have security zones. Naval vessel protection zones direct boaters to stay at least 100 yards away from all large naval vessels (unless directed to approach) as well as installations, piers, and other security zones. Make sure you know about local restrictions, too. Help keep America safe.

Kayaking on Lakes and State Waterways

Many lakes and rivers are marked with information and regulatory signs and buoys indicating restricted or hazardous areas. It's important to keep in mind that not all hazards are marked. The safe paddler always obeys these signs:.

Controlled Area.
Look in the circle for further information. These are found at speed zones, no-fishing areas, no-anchoring areas, ski zones, no-wake zones, etc.

Danger—Use Caution.
This may mark construction areas, reefs, shoals, or sunken objects.

Boats Keep Out.
The nature of the danger may be placed around the outside of the crossed diamond. These may mark waterfalls, dams, swim areas, or rapids.

Information.
These tell directions, distances, and other non-regulatory messages.

WARNING!

Do not approach within 100 yards of any U.S. naval vessel. If you need to pass within 100 yards of a U.S. naval vessel in order to ensure a safe passage in accordance with the Navigation Rules, you must contact the U.S. naval vessel or the Coast Guard escort vessel on VHF-FM channel 16.

You must operate at minimum speed within 500 yards of any U.S. naval vessel and proceed as directed by the Commanding Officer or the official patrol.

Violations of the Naval Vessel Protection Zone are a felony offense, punishable by up to six years in prison and/or up to $250,000 in fines.

Glossary of Terms

Abeam: At a right angle to the keel line.
Afloat: On the water.
Aft: A term describing direction toward the rear or stern of a boat.
Aground: Touching bottom.
Amidship: Describing the midsection of a vessel.
Astern: Aft or toward the stern.

Backband (*back rest*): Provides support for the lower back while kayaking and helps with erect posture in the boat. Located behind the seat and usually made of padded fabric, plastic, or foam.
Backface: The side of the paddle blade opposite the powerface.
Beam: Vessel's width amidship.
Blade: The broad part at the ends of the paddle.
Boil: A mound of water deflected up by underwater obstructions.
Bow: The forward end of the boat.
Bracing stroke: Used to help a paddler regain balance. Can be dangerous if performed with poor technique. For this reason it is considered a more advanced stroke, requiring personal instruction.
Broach: To be turned broadside by wind, wave, or current.
Bulkhead: A cross-sectional wall inside a kayak, made of composite, plastic, or foam. Bulkheads provide structural support and, if sealed around the inside of the hull, can create watertight compartments for buoyancy and storage. They are sometimes also used as foot braces.

Capsize: To turn the kayak over in the water.
Catch: The part of a paddle stroke placing the blade in the water.
Channel: A route through obstructions or shallows. Often marked with buoys or marker lights.
Chine: The transition from hull sidewall to bottom.
Cockpit: The enclosed central compartment on a kayak, in which the paddler sits.
Control hand: Hand used to twist the paddle shaft so as to use offset blades.

Deck: The top part of a kayak that keeps the hull from filling with water.
Draft: The depth of water a kayak draws.

Eddy: The area behind an obstruction in current with still water or upstream current.
Eddy line: The line that separates the eddy from the main current.

Falls: Drops where water falls free.
Feather: To slice or move the paddle edgewise, thus reducing the drag caused by air or water during recovery phase.
Ferry: Maneuver in which a paddler uses the force of the water to move the kayak sideways across the current.
Flatwater: Lakes, protected bays or sea, or a calm river without rapids.
Flotation: Waterproof compartments, foam blocks, or inflatable air bags. This flotation will help a swamped boat stay on the surface, making rescue and reentry easier.
Foot pegs (*foot braces*): Usually adjustable structures inside the cockpit on which a kayaker places the balls of his/her feet. *See* "Bulkhead."
Freeboard: The amount of kayak hull above the waterline.

Hull: The structural body of the boat, the shape of which determines how the boat will perform.

Hydraulic: Turbulence caused by water flowing over an obstacle.
Hypothermia: Physical condition that occurs when the body loses heat faster than it can produce it.

Keel: The longitudinal centerline of the kayak.
Keeper: A hydraulic that holds objects in recirculating water.

Ledge: A projecting rock layer partially damming water flow.
Low-head dam: A fixed obstruction across a stream or river in which water drops over the crest creating a hydraulic that can trap and recirculate objects.

Pack canoes: Small canoes paddled like kayaks with double-blade paddles.
Paddle float: An inflatable float that can be attached to one paddle blade. Used to aid deep-water reentry.
Peelout: Turning downstream from an eddy.
PFD: Personal flotation device. Cushions, and most importantly for kayakers, life jackets. PFDs used in the United States must be U.S. Coast Guard approved and must be worn to be effective. The Coast Guard recognizes five types of PFDs. These must be used in accordance with the label. Kayakers most commonly use Type IIIs.
Powerface: The face of the blade that pushes against the water on the forward stroke.
Pump: A small device used to bail or empty a swamped kayak.

Rapids: River section with steep, fast flow around obstructions.
Recovery: Moving the paddle from stroke end to the next catch.
Rescue sling: A loop of rope or webbing used to aid reentry.
Riffles: Water flow across shallows causing small waves.
Rocker: The upturn of the kayak's keel line at either end of the hull. More bow rocker (more curvature) usually makes a kayak more maneuverable. Less stern rocker tends to help the kayak track in a straight line.
Roll: The technique of righting a capsized kayak with the paddler remaining in the paddling position.
Rudder: A controllable fin mounted at the kayak's stern to aid tracking and turning.
Rudder stroke: Drawing in or pushing away a paddle blade placed near the stern. Used to control the kayak's direction.

Sea kayak: Long slender kayaks, usually used with spray skirts. Most modern designs have bulkheads forming waterproof compartments. Hatches to these compartments provide easy access for stowing equipment, camping gear, etc.
Shaft: The long skinny part of a kayak paddle.
Sit-on-top: Kayaks without a cockpit, sit-on-tops are usually self-bailing with various seat and foot brace configurations. Many are for recreational use, but some are designed for touring or racing.
Skeg: A fin mounted near the stern along the keel line that aids tracking.
Slack water: Water flowing without riffles or rapids.
Slice: Edgewise movement of the paddle blade through water.

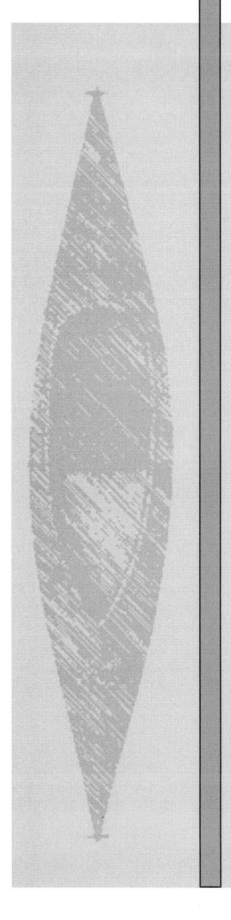

Spray skirt *(deck):* A neoprene or nylon skirt worn by a kayaker that attaches to the rim (coaming) of the cockpit. It keeps water out of the kayak.

Stern: The rear end of the kayak.

Stow: To secure gear in a boat.

Strainer: An obstruction in moving water which allows water to pass through but stops and hold objects such as boats and people. Fallen trees often form strainers in current, as do docks and piers.

Swamp: To fill (a kayak) with water.

Sweep boat: The assigned last kayak in a group of paddlers.

Thigh braces *(knee braces):* Usually found in whitewater and high-performance touring kayaks, these structures inside the cockpit give the paddler points of contact important for boat control.

Throat: The transitional area where paddle blade and shaft meet.

Tip: The extreme end of the paddle blade, or alternatively, to turn a boat over.

Track: The tendency for a kayak to run on course. See Rocker, Rudder, and Skeg.

Trim: The bow-to-stern leveling of a kayak that affects boat control. In most cases it should be nearly level, or with the stern slightly lower in the water.

Trip leader: An experienced and qualified paddler leading the group on an outing.

Trough: The depression between waves.

Upstream V: Formed by an obstruction in current which creates a **V** that points upstream.

Waterline: The intersection of hull and water surface.

Wet exit: Coming out of a capsized kayak.

Whitewater: Aerated rapids.

YOUR BOATING
DOLLARS AT WORK

Funding Provided by a Grant from the Sport Fish Restoration and Boating Trust Fund Administered by the U.S. Coast Guard

KNOW YOUR LIMITS

AMERICAN CANOE ASSOCIATION
Kayak & Canoe Recreation

A SPECIAL SAFETY PUBLICATION FROM THE AMERICAN CANOE ASSOCIATION.

YOUR BOATING
DOLLARS AT WORK

PRODUCED UNDER A GRANT FROM THE SPORT FISH RESTORATION AND BOATING TRUST FUND, ADMINISTERED BY THE U.S. COAST GUARD.

Paddle Smart ...
Know Your Limits

MORE AND MORE PEOPLE ARE GETTING INTO PADDLING. ACCORDING TO A 2006 STUDY BY THE OUTDOOR INDUSTRY FOUNDATION, AMERICANS ARE PADDLING IN RECORD NUMBERS: 20-22 MILLION PADDLED A CANOE, 20-22 MILLION WENT RAFTING AND 10-12 MILLION KAYAKED IN 2005. THE NUMBER OF KAYAKERS REPRESENTS A 272% GROWTH DURING THE STUDY'S FIVE-YEAR PERIOD. THIS GROWTH IS NOT SURPRISING SINCE PADDLING IS A PERFECT WAY TO ENJOY THE OUTDOORS, HAVE SOME FUN AND STAY IN SHAPE.

ALSO NOT SURPRISING, AS PADDLING HAS grown, so has the number of paddlesport-related, on-water accidents. Nearly 75% of those who die in paddlesport-related accidents were not wearing a lifejacket. Alcohol use was also a contributing factor in almost 20% of the cases. Hazardous water or weather conditions are cited as the primary cause in more than 40% of fatal paddlesport accidents.

What do these different risk factors have in common? They are all things that a smart paddler can plan for and, in almost every case, avoid! By recognizing and accepting responsibility for the potential risks you face when you take to the water in a canoe, kayak or raft, you can eliminate or at least greatly minimize the chances of an on-water accident. There is MUCH you can do

to manage the risks, including pre-trip preparation and planning, personal and equipment preparation, and most importantly being safety conscious while on the water and at the put-in and take-out.

This paddlesport safety section has been produced by the American Canoe Association under a grant from the Sport Fish Restoration and Boating Trust Fund administered by the U.S. Coast Guard, as a basic safety primer for use by all paddlers, old pros and novices alike. But it takes more than just reading about types of paddlecraft for all levels of experience at locations across the country. Check out the ACA website (www.americancanoe.org) for more information on paddling courses in your area.

Most people feel that safety is a concern for

the other guy. "It will never happen to me." While paddling is a relatively safe recreational activity when considering its immense popularity, it can also appear deceptively easy and safe – and not just to novice paddlers. Operator inexperience or error is indicated as a leading cause of only about one in four paddlesport fatalities, and about one-third of all fatalities, where experience was reported, are of paddlers with more than 100 hours of experience.

So regardless of your level of experience – whether you are just starting out or have been paddling your whole life – Know Your Limits and always follow the basic safety precautions described in the following pages.

Paddle Safe and Paddle Often!

YOUR BOATING DOLLARS AT WORK

PRODUCED UNDER A GRANT FROM THE SPORT FISH RESTORATION AND BOATING TRUST FUND, ADMINISTERED BY THE U.S. COAST GUARD.

Wear Your Lifejacket!

EXPECT TO CAPSIZE AND SWIM OCCASIONALLY when paddling a canoe, kayak, or raft — it's part of the fun! But when you hit the water unexpectedly, even strong swimmers need a Personal Flotation Device (PFD), commonly called a "lifejacket." It allows you to concentrate on doing what's needed to increase your safety and improve your chances of rescue. Over 75% of all drownings involving canoes, kayaks or rafts would never have happened if the victim had been wearing a lifejacket!

Many people think a lifejacket has to be bulky and uncomfortable, but this isn't true any more. The U.S. Coast Guard places PFDs into five categories.

Type I or II PFDs are safe and will turn an unconscious person face up, but they are generally too bulky for paddlers.

Type III PFDs are designed to be worn all the time. They come in a wide variety of designs, colors and prices. Lifejackets for most paddlers fall into this category. Their minimum buoyancy is 15.5 pounds, although a few models are available with higher flotation (used primarily for very large paddlers).

Type IV PFDs cover a variety of "throwable devices," like ring buoys and seat cushions.

Type V covers a variety of "special purpose" PFDs, including whitewater rescue lifejackets, PFDs used by commercial rafters and even a new breed of inflatable lifejackets (low-profile PFDs built for comfort, but not approved for use in whitewater).

Because paddlers wear their lifejackets all day, make sure yours has a secure yet comfortable fit. When wearing the right lifejacket you'll hardly know you have it on.

Although all approved Type III PFDs meet certain strength and buoyancy standards, they're not all the same. Spend some extra money for a higher-quality model. It will have softer foam, a more comfortable cut, and improved adjustability. Make sure your lifejacket adjusts easily and fits snugly over clothing worn for different weather conditions.

Few universal-sized lifejackets fit as well as models sized small, medium, large and extra large. Very large men will need an XXL version. Check the length to be sure that your lifejacket will be out of the way when paddling.

Women and kids can be hard to fit. Women are smaller and shaped differently than men. They also have shorter torsos, making many unisex PFDs too long. Fortunately, several companies have designed special ladies' models that fit well.

Kids also require specially sized lifejackets. You should be able to lift children by their lifejackets without having them fall out. With very young children with flat torsos, a crotch strap is a good idea to help hold the lifejacket in place. The Coast Guard places kids less than 90 pounds into a separate sizing category; if a child is heavier than that, look for an extra-small adult jacket.

Most importantly, although many PFDs are sold in sizes such as small, medium, large, etc., the correct size is always dependent on the wearer's weight. Chest size and fit is very important, but so is the correct size by weight. Always check the PFD's label for size/weight limits and specifications.

LIFEJACKETS MATTER!
Consider the following statistics:
* 98% of all canoe/kayak operators had a PFD with them
* 63% of all paddlecraft operators wore their PFD all or most of the time
** 75% of all canoe/kayak fatalities were not wearing a PFD

*Source: 1998 National Recreational Boating Survey, conducted by JSI Research and Training Institute, Inc.
** Source: 1999 U.S. Coast Guard Boating Statistics

PHOTO BY ISTOCKPHOTO © ANSSI RUUSKA

Avoid Extremes of Weather and Water

FOR PADDLERS WHO WEAR LIFEJACKETS, EXTREME WEATHER AND WATER CONDITIONS ARE THE USUAL COURSE OF TROUBLE. IF YOU ENCOUNTER THESE CONDITIONS, STAY OFF THE WATER. SKILLED PADDLERS WITH PROPER GEAR CAN HANDLE SOME EXTREMES SAFELY, BUT EVEN THEY KNOW WHEN TO BACK OFF. HERE ARE SOME THINGS TO KNOW ABOUT:

COLD WATER

Cold water is extremely dangerous. It quickly robs the body of its strength, diminishes coordination and impairs judgment. Immersion in water as warm as 50-60 degrees can initiate what has been determined to be "Cold Water Shock." When a paddler capsizes and is suddenly immersed in cold water the body's first reflexive action is to gasp for air, followed by increased heart rate, blood pressure and disorientation, and can even lead to cardiac arrest. Without proper equipment and apparel, the body can become incapacitated in just a few minutes, and without a lifejacket this can be a very dangerous and often fatal combination. When paddling in places where the water temperature is 60 degrees Fahrenheit or colder, a wetsuit is a must and a drysuit is highly recommended. This is also the case if the combined air and water temperatures are below 120 degrees Fahrenheit.

Another dangerous situation that can occur in cold water or cold weather is hypothermia. Hypothermia occurs when exposure to the elements prohibits the body from reheating and maintaining its core temperature. Typical symptoms of hypothermia include: shivering, impaired judgment, clumsiness, loss of manual dexterity, and slurred speech.

Methods of treatment for cold water shock and hypothermia vary depending on the severity of the situation. The most important thing to remember is that the individual in either of these situations needs to be warmed slowly.

STEPS TO PROTECT AGAINST THE EFFECTS OF COLD WATER

• Select and layer clothing properly
• Have spare clothing available in a sealed dry bag while on the water
• Always wear your lifejacket
• Keep yourself well-hydrated and fueled with high-carbohydrate foods

HIGH WATER

High water makes a river move faster and with much greater force, adding power to even the mildest drop. As river current gains speed, rescue becomes more difficult. As a river floods, water spills over the banks and can rush through surrounding trees and brush, creating strainers. Rivers rise and fall with the seasons, and the flow varies with rain and snowmelt. Fluctuations from a few feet to as much as ten feet are not uncommon. The river you ran last year, or even last week may be completely different when you return. Know what the river level is and what it means to paddlers before you get out on the water.

HIGH WINDS AND STORMS

High Winds and Storms over open water turn the placid surface of a lake or bay into a wild, unfriendly place. The bigger the body of water, the rougher it can get. Experienced lake and coastal paddlers monitor the weather closely, checking forecasts beforehand and watching the sky when on the water. A knowledgeable and safe paddler is not afraid to postpone a trip if necessary, or to head for shore if conditions start to deteriorate.

INTERNATIONAL SCALE OF RIVER DIFFICULTY

The following rapid-rating scale is only a guide and is often interpreted differently by different people. Since many rivers don't fit neatly into a system, check several sources before assuming you have the ability to run the sections. Fluctuating water levels caused by rainfall or river releases may change the class rating. Temperatures below 50 degrees F should change a rating to be one class more difficult than normal.

Class I – Easy
Moving water with a few riffles and small waves. Few or no obstructions

Class II – Novice
Easy rapids with waves up to three feet and wide, clear channels that are obvious without scouting. Some maneuvering is required.

Class III – Intermediate
Rapids with high, irregular waves often capable of swamping an open canoe. Narrow passages that often require complex maneuvering. May require some scouting from shore.

Class IV – Advanced
Long, difficult rapids and constricted passages that often require precise maneuvering in very turbulent waters. Scouting from shore is often necessary, and conditions make rescue difficult. Canoeists and kayakers should have a reliable roll.

Class V – Expert
Extremely difficult. Long, very violent rapids with highly congested routes, which nearly always must be scouted from shore. Rescue conditions are difficult, and there is a significant hazard to life in the event of a mishap. Ability to roll is essential for all boaters.

Class VI – Extreme and Exploratory Rapid
Difficulties of Class V carried to the extreme of navigability. Nearly impossible and very dangerous. For teams of experts only, after close study has been made and all precautions have been taken.
Source: American Whitewater

DID YOU KNOW?

• Not wearing a lifejacket in a boat is like not wearing a seatbelt in a car. When you need it, it is too late!
• Many boat-related fatalities involve alcohol. Stay sober and stay alive.
• Standing up in swift current is dangerous. If your foot gets trapped under a rock or root, the force of the water can push you over and hold you under the surface. Keep your feet up!
• Paddlers don't often notice they are thirsty when having fun on the water. Take plenty of potable water with you and drink frequently.
• The body loses heat 30 times faster when immersed in water. Dress for immersion – plan on it.

YOUR BOATING
DOLLARS AT WORK

PRODUCED UNDER A GRANT FROM THE SPORT FISH RESTORATION AND BOATING TRUST FUND, ADMINISTERED BY THE U.S. COAST GUARD.

Safety Tidbits

UNIVERSAL RIVER SIGNALS

Stop: Potential hazard ahead. Wait for "all clear" signals before proceeding or scout ahead. Form a horizontal bar with your paddle or outstretched arms. Those seeing the signal should pass it to others in the party.

Help/Emergency: Assist the signaler as quickly as possible. Give three long blasts on a whistle while waving a paddle, helmet or PFD over your head in a circular motion. If a whistle is not available, use the visual signal alone. A whistle is best attached to the zipper of the PFD.

All Clear: Come ahead (in the absence of other directions, proceed down the center). Form a vertical bar with your paddle or one arm held high above your head. The paddle blade should be turned flat for maximum visibility. To signal direction or a preferred course through a rapid around an obstruction, lower the previously vertical "all clear" by 45 degrees toward the side of the river with the preferred route. Never point toward the object you wish to avoid

(Source: American Whitewater).

SPOTTING A POTENTIAL ACCIDENT

Accidents don't just happen. They usually result from the interaction of a series of smaller events or misjudgments, which culminate in a major accident. Experts analyze accidents in terms of their human, equipment and environmental factors. Usually, any one factor will not lead to an accident. However, the presence of three or more factors in a paddling situation is a sign of serious trouble.

Human Factors:
1. Consumption of alcohol
2. Not wearing a lifejacket
3. Lack of familiarity with river
4. Insufficient skill level
5. Being out of shape
6. Paddling alone or in a group with less than three boats

Equipment Factors:
1. Poorly maintained equipment (i.e. cracked paddles, leaky rafts)
2. Little or no flotation
3. No spare paddle
4. No first aid kit
5. Improper or inadequate dress

Environmental Factors
1. High water
2. Cold water
3. Dams (hydraulics)
4. Strainers (downed trees)
5. Undercut rocks
6. Remoteness
7. Changing weather conditions

THROW ROPE BAG

The throw rope bag is a rescue device that can be thrown quickly to a swimmer or used to unpin a boat. It can be easily stored in a boat ready for quick use. It should contain between 50 and 70 feet of 3/8" soft-braided polypropylene rope, stuffed randomly into the bag and extending through the bag to form a loop. When throwing the bag, first loosen the drawstring. Hold the end loop in one hand (don't put your hand in the loop) and throw the bag at or behind the victim in the rapids. A second bag works best if you miss with the first. If you have only one bag and have another chance to make a throw, drop the rope as it lies at your feet when you retrieve it. Leave some water in the bag for ballast and throw it again to the victim. If the victim grabs the rope, "belay" yourself (sit down, brace yourself and run the rope behind your hip) and let the victim swing to shore.

SELF RESCUE

When spilled, check on your partner, get to the upstream end of the craft and swim to the safest shore (a 15-foot canoe hurled against a rock by a current of 10mph can exert a force of over four tons). Leave the boat only if it will improve your personal safety. If a rescue is not imminent, if the water is numbing cold or if a worse set of rapids is approaching, strike out for the safest shore. To lessen your chance of injury, adopt the safe swim position by floating on your back with your feet pointing downstream and at the surface of the water. Don't attempt standing in moving water at knee-deep levels or deeper because of the possibility of foot entrapment, even in relatively slow-moving water. Many drownings have occurred when a novice paddler has had a foot or leg caught between rocks in a strong current.

LAYERING YOUR CLOTHES

Layered clothes insulate in cool weather better than a single garment of the same thickness (two medium-weight sweaters offer more protection than one heavy sweater). Cover the sweaters with a paddling jacket for more warmth. To trap heat and keep water out, the paddling jacket should fit tightly around the neck, wrists and waist. Layers can be mixed to maximize the strengths of each layer. Some paddlers use a farmer john-type wetsuit (no sleeves) coupled with a sweater and paddling jacket, allowing freedom of movement and extra protection while swimming. The layering system also allows you to easily adjust your body temperature.

PARTICIPANTS' PREPAREDNESS AND RESPONSIBILITY

1. Be a competent swimmer with the ability to handle yourself underwater and in moving water.
2. Be certain to have a properly fitting lifejacket and WEAR IT.
3. Be suitably equipped.
4. Keep craft under control (control must be good enough at all times to stop or reach shore before reaching any danger). Know your boating ability. Don't enter a rapid unless you're reasonably sure you can safely navigate it or swim the entire rapid in the event of capsizing.

KNOW CPR

Cardio Pulmonary Resuscitation (CPR) is an emergency first aid procedure that allows the rescuer to maintain life until a victim recovers sufficiently to be transported, or until advanced life support is available. It involves recognizing respiratory and cardio arrest and starting the proper application or resuscitation. CPR procedures following a near drowning should be performed as quickly as possible. Optimally, only seconds should intervene between recognizing the need and starting treatment. CPR is a basic form of life support that can be taught to anyone. If you've been trained in CRP, review it periodically and make sure your registration is current. If you haven't, contact your local Red Cross as to when to enroll in the next course. Your paddling partner's life could depend on it.

PHOTO BY CHRISTIAN KNIGHT

PRODUCED UNDER A GRANT FROM THE SPORT FISH RESTORATION AND BOATING TRUST FUND. ADMINISTERED BY THE U.S. COAST GUARD.

YOUR BOATING DOLLARS AT WORK

Safety Tips For

TOURING/COASTAL KAYAKING

ESSENTIAL EQUIPMENT

TOURING
Sun hat
UV-protection eyewear
Lifejacket
Spare paddle
Sunscreen
Water bottle

WHITEWATER
Helmet
Lifejacket
Whistle
River knife
Throw rope
Appropriate clothing
Dry bag (with first aid kit)

OTHER SAFETY EQUIPMENT

SEA KAYAKING
Bilge pump, paddle float, sling, sponsons or other self-rescue device, map/chart and compass, signal mirror, tow line

RAFTING
Patch kit, (with glue, patch material and scissors), pump, spare lifejacket, wrap pulley system, bow line, footwear for scouting/portaging

CANOEING
Bail bucket, float bags and pulley system (for whitewater), painter lines

WHITEWATER KAYAKING
Footwear for scouting/portaging, float bags, bulkhead or beam, dry bag with spare clothes, breakdown paddle, z-drag system, rescue harness

• **LEARN RE-ENTRY, AND PRACTICE IN CONTROLLED CONDITIONS**
Slide your belly across the boat, then your butt, then your legs
Assisted rescue
Paddle float for decked kayaks

• **KNOW YOUR HAZARDS**
Tidal currents
Landings in surf
Other traffic

• **KEEP YOUR GROUP CLOSE TOGETHER**
File a float plan

• **CHOOSE A ROUTE**
Close to shore
Without fast currents
With protected coastlines and surf under one foot

• **CHECK THE WEATHER AND OTHER LOCAL CONDITIONS**
Fog
Wind

• **DRESS FOR AN UNEXPECTED FLIP**
Hypothermia is a serious threat in kayak touring—wear a wet suit or other protective clothing
Wear your PFD-fastened and snug

PHOTOS BY CHRISTIAN KNIGHT

All Disciplines

ABOVE PHOTO BY ISTOCKPHOTO © MICHAEL OLSON/ ANGEL HERRERO DE FRUTOS

WHITEWATER KAYAKING & RAFTING

• PICK AN APPROPRIATE RIVER

Match your skills and experience to the difficulty of the river

• USE PROPER EQUIPMENT

Lifejacket–fastened and snug
Helmet–use varies by river difficulty, water level, and local custom
Adequate flotation for kayaks and canoes
No loose lines; avoid entanglement
Protective footwear and cold water protection

• RECOGNIZE AND AVOID HAZARDS

Trees, branches and other strainers
Rocks and low-head dams
Backwash in hydraulics
Stay on the inside of bends

• SWIM AGGRESSIVELY

Away from hazards (toward calm water, shore or your raft)
If rafting, pull swimmers aboard immediately

• DEFENSIVELY SWIM

Feet up and pointed downstream
Backstroke to maneuver
Don't stand up

• IF IN DOUBT, GET OUT AND SCOUT

Walk or carry around danger spots
Keep your group close together

CANOEING

• CHOOSE AN APPROPRIATE LAKE OR RIVER

Cross big lakes and run swift rivers only if you have the necessary skills

• HAZARDS CAN EXIST EVEN ON QUIET WATER

Watch for changing weather and water conditions
Keep an eye out for other boat traffic
Pay attention to all safety warnings

• WEAR THE RIGHT GEAR

Keep your PFD fastened and snug
Wear appropriate clothing for the conditions
Keep your shoes on–sharp objects abound near shore

• TAKE THE RIGHT EQUIPMENT

Make sure you take plenty of water and food
Carry lights if you'll be out in low light conditions
Carry an extra paddle
Carry flotation if you're paddling whitewater

YOUR BOATING
DOLLARS AT WORK

PRODUCED UNDER A GRANT FROM THE SPORT FISH RESTORATION AND BOATING TRUST FUND. ADMINISTERED BY THE U.S. COAST GUARD.

Safety Resources for Paddlers

LOOKING FOR MORE INFORMATION ON PADDLESPORTS SAFETY? CONTACT ANY OF THE FOLLOWING ORGANIZATIONS FOR MORE ADVICE ON PADDLING AND SAFETY:

AMERICAN CANOE ASSOCIATION
1340 Central Park Blvd., #210
Fredericksburg, VA 22401
540-907-4460; www.americancanoe.org

AMERICA OUTDOORS
PO Box 10847, Knoxville, TN 37939
865-558-3595; www.americaoutdoors.org

AMERICAN WHITEWATER
1430 Fenwick Lane, Silver Spring, MD 20910
301-589-9453; www.americanwhitewater.org

PADDLESPORTS INDUSTRY ASSOCIATION
PO Box 7189 Silver Spring, MD 20907
703-451-3864; www.paddlesportsindustry.org

TRADE ASSOCIATION OF PADDLESPORTS
PO Box 243
Milner, BC Canada, V0X-1T0
(800) 755-5228; www.gopaddle.org

UNITED STATES CANOE ASSOCIATION
606 Ross. St. Middletown, OH 45044-5062
513-422-3739; www.uscanoe.com

USA CANOE AND KAYAK
301 South Tryon Street, Suite 1750 Charlotte, NC 28282
704-348-4330; www.usack.org

THE FOLLOWING ORGANIZATIONS PROVIDE GENERAL INFORMATION ON BOATING SAFETY:

UNITED STATES COAST GUARD-OFFICE OF BOATING SAFETY
www.uscgboating.org

UNITED STATES COAST GUARD AUXILLARY
www.cgaux.org

NATIONAL ASSOCIATION OF STATE BOATING LAW ADMINISTRATORS
www.nasbla.org

NATIONAL SAFE BOATING COUNCIL
www.safeboatingcouncil.org

UNITED STATES ARMY CORPS OF ENGINEERS
www.usace.army.mil

PHOTO BY ISTOCKPHOTO.COM © BEAT GLAUSER